SCHIRMER'S LIBRARY
OF MUSICAL CLASSICS

Vol. 2001

SERGEI RACHMANINOFF

Complete Preludes for Piano

Op. 3, 23, 32

ISBN 978-0-7935-3306-0

G. SCHIRMER, *Inc.*

DISTRIBUTED BY

7777 W. BLUEMOUND RD. P.O. BOX 13819 MILWAUKEE, WI 53213

CONTENTS

Edited and fingered by
Louis Oesterle

Prélude

S.RACHMANINOFF. Op.3, № 2

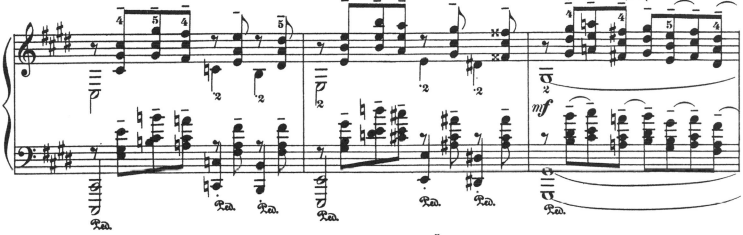

Agitato

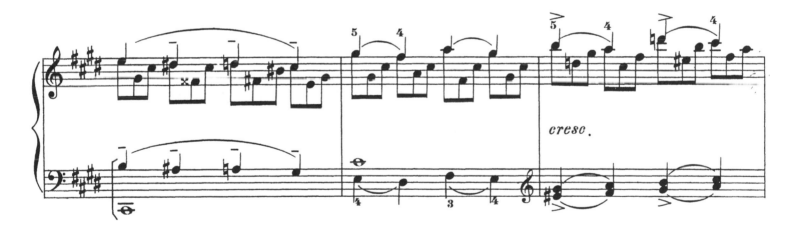

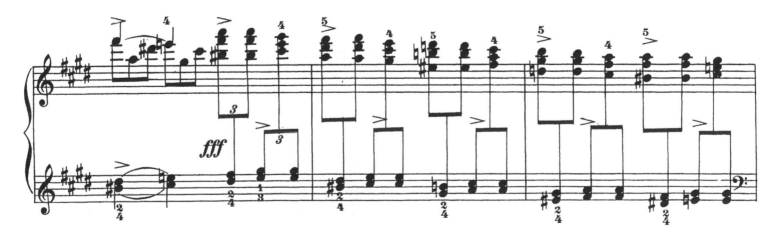

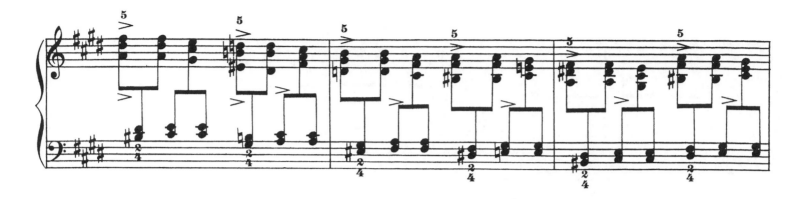

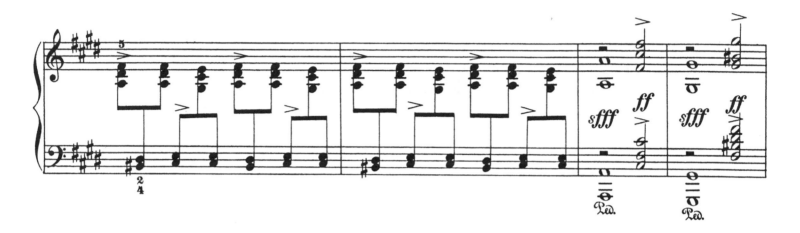

Tempo I

I

S. Rachmaninoff, Op. 23, № 1.

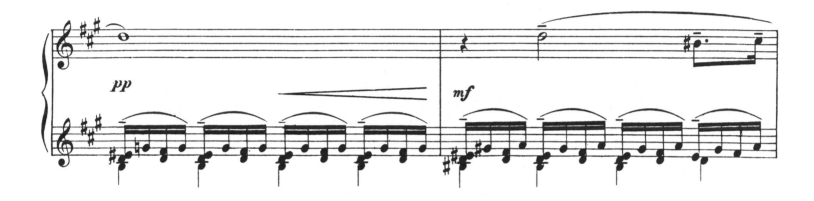

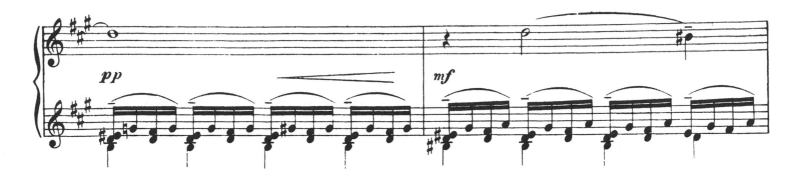

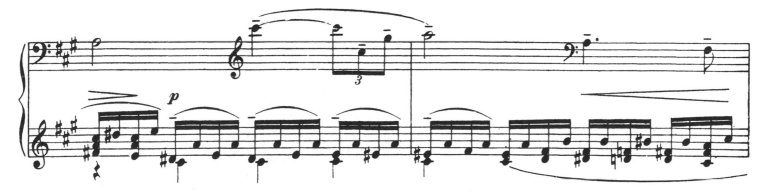

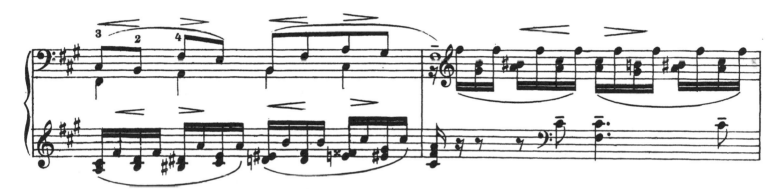

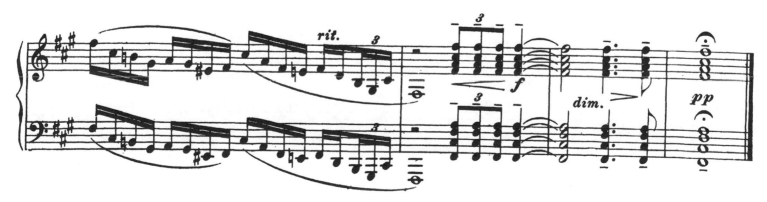

10

II

S. Rachmaninoff, Op. 23, № 2

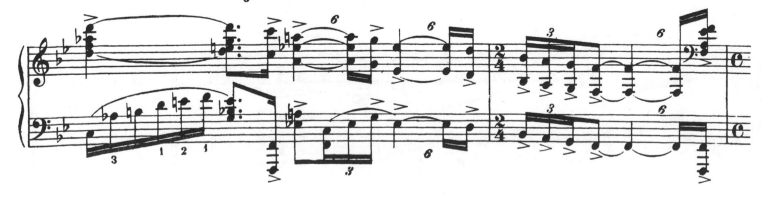

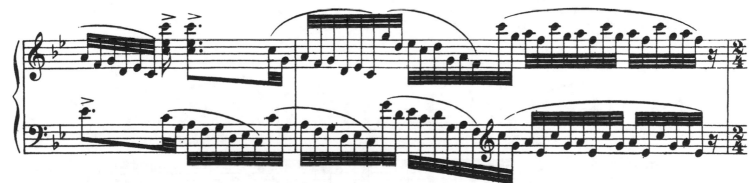

III

S. Rachmaninoff, Op. 23, № 3.

Tempo di minuetto (♩ = 66)

Tempo I

IV

S. Rachmaninoff, Op. 23, № 4.

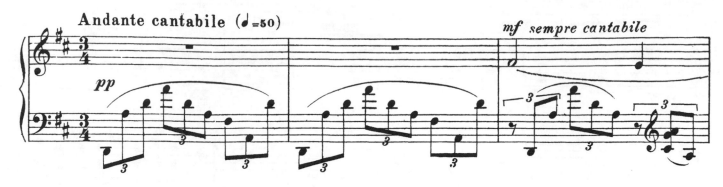

a tempo

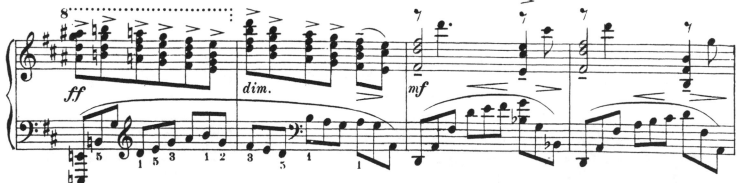

V

S. Rachmaninoff, Op. 23, № 5

Alla marcia ($\quad$=108)

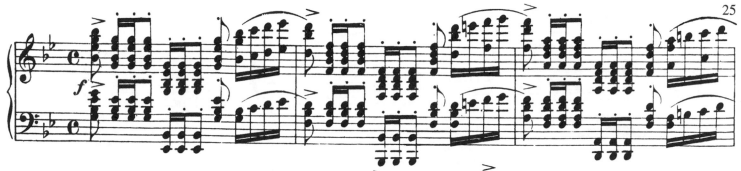

Un poco meno mosso

poco a poco accelerando e cresc. al Tempo I

Tempo I

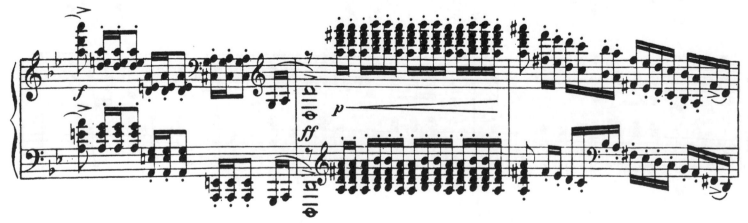

VI

S. Rachmaninoff, Op. 23, № 6.

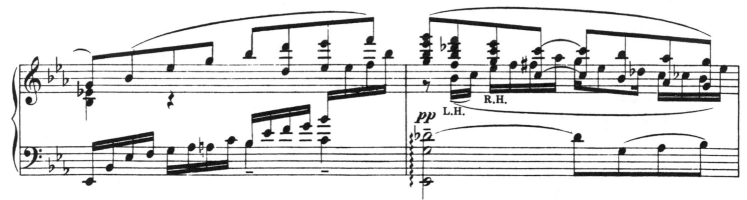

VII

S. Rachmaninoff, Op. 23. № 7.

Allegro (♩=80)

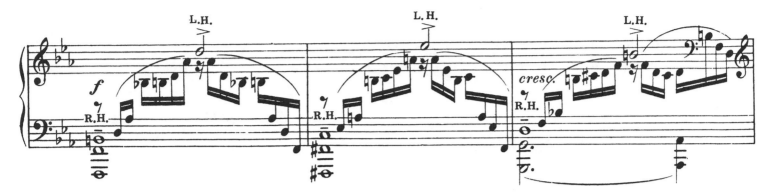

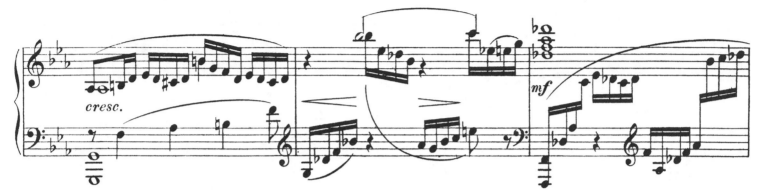

VIII

S. Rachmaninoff, Op. 23, № 8.

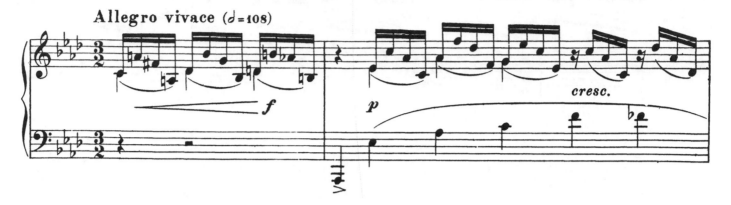

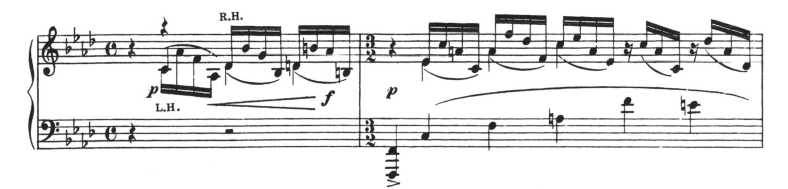

IX

S. Rachmaninoff, Op. 23, № 9.

49

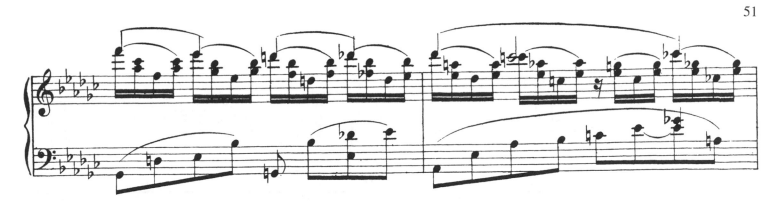

X

S. Rachmaninoff, Op. 23, № 10

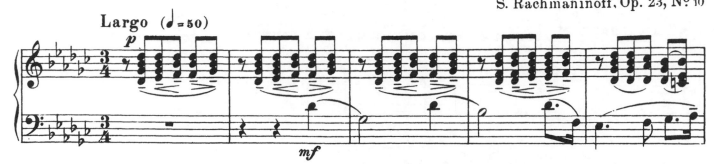

poco a poco cresc. ed accel.

I

S. Rachmaninoff, Op. 32, № 1.

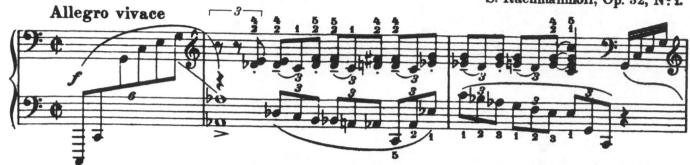

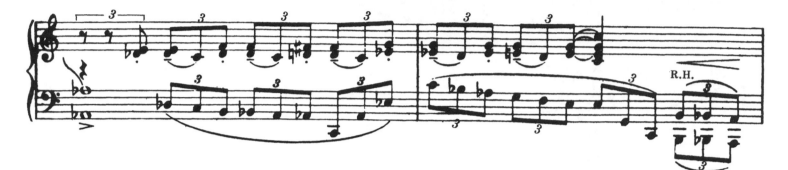

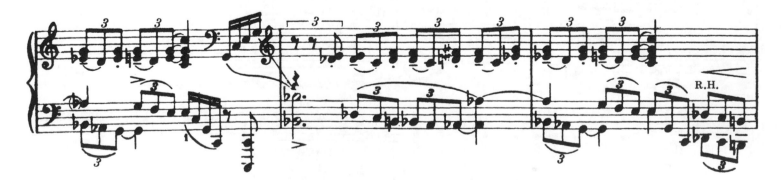

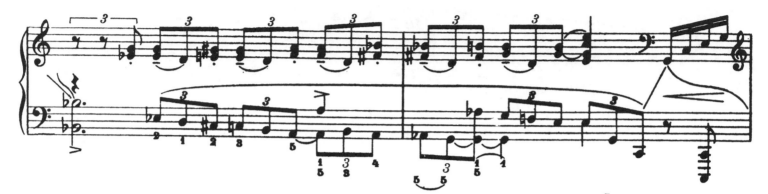

II

S. Rachmaninoff. Op. 32, No. 2.

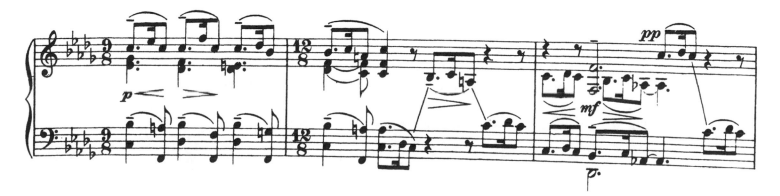

Allegro

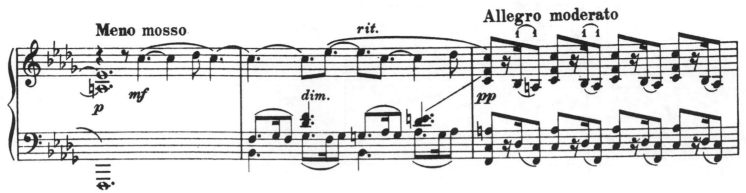

III

Allegro vivace

S. Rachmaninoff. Op. 32, Nº 3.

sempre marcato

poco a poco dim.

p

dim.

pp

rit.

Meno mosso

IV

Allegro con brio

S. Rachmaninoff, Op. 32. N? 4.

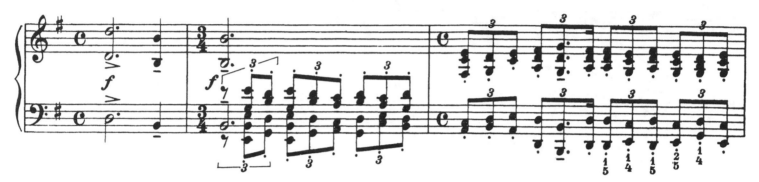

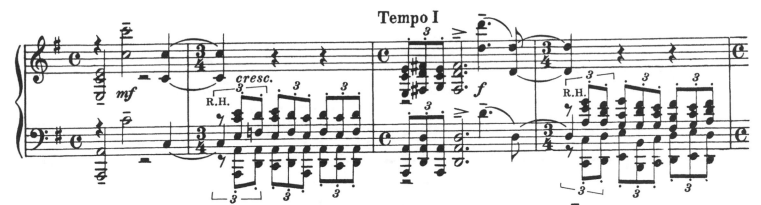

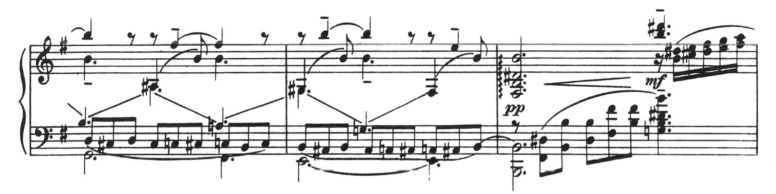

Tempo I

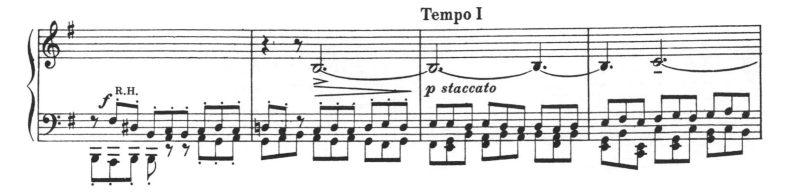

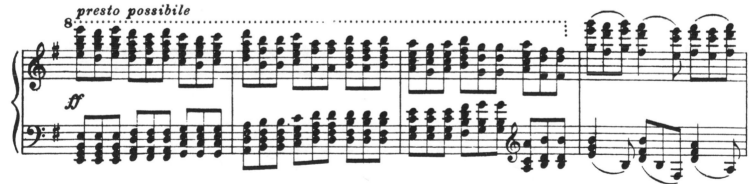

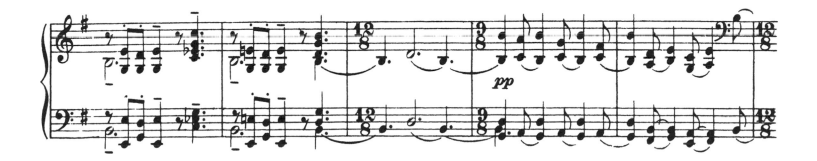

V

S. Rachmaninoff, Op. 32. Nº 5.

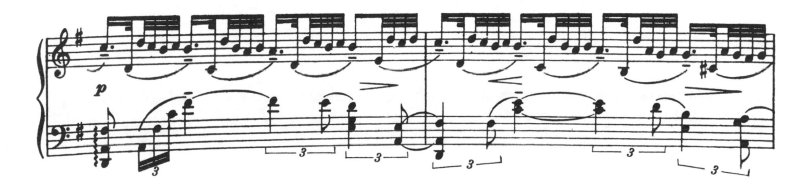

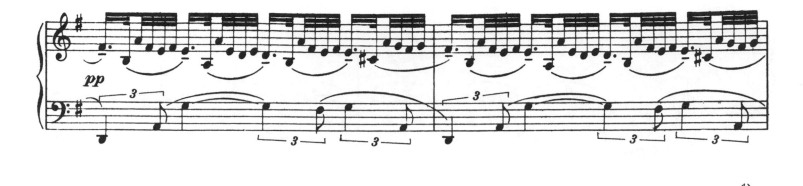

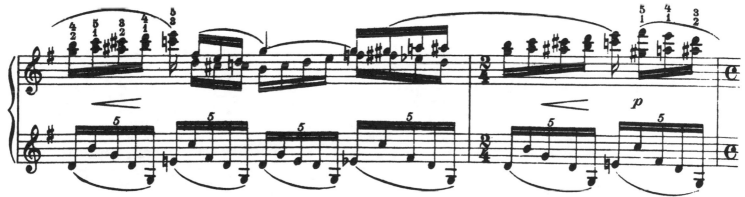

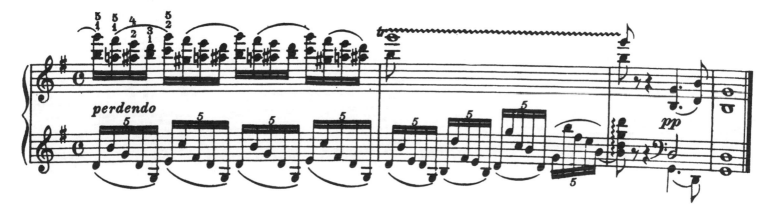

VI

S. Rachmaninoff, Op. 32. № 6.

Allegro appassionato

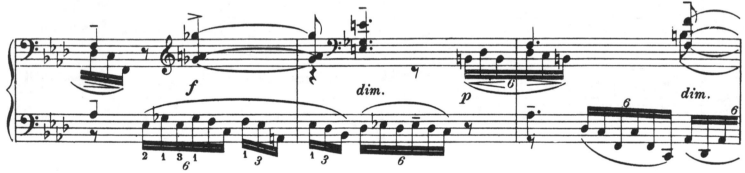

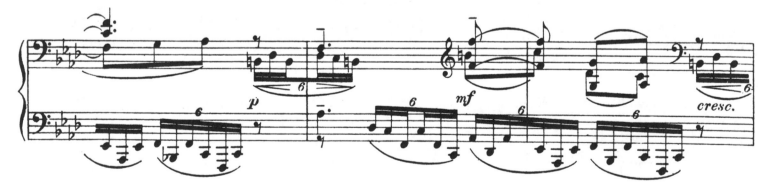

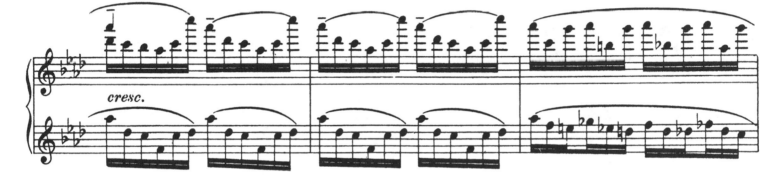

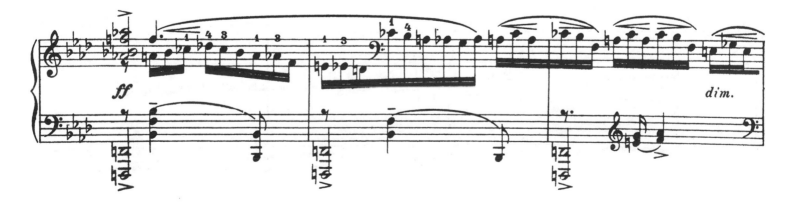

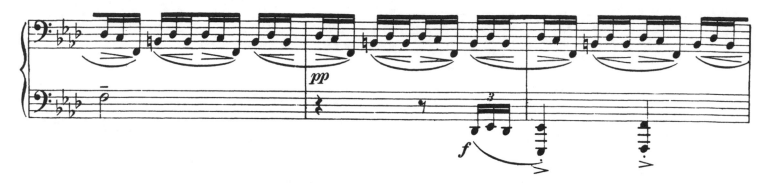

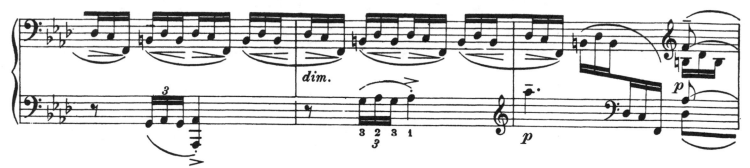

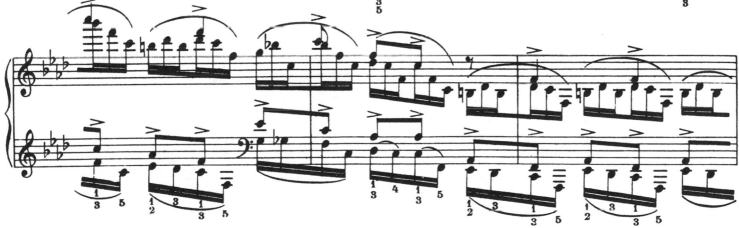

VII

S. Rachmaninoff, Op.32.№7.

a tempo

Più vivo

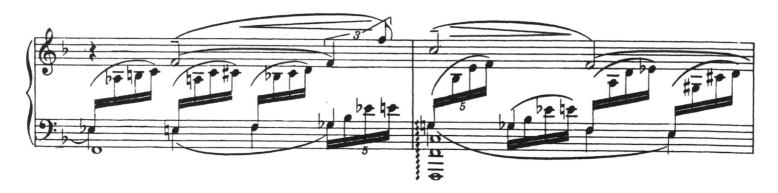

VIII

S. Rachmaninoff, Op. 32. N°8.

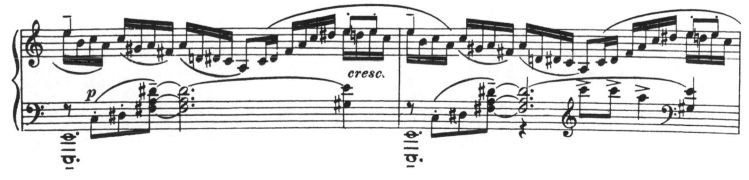

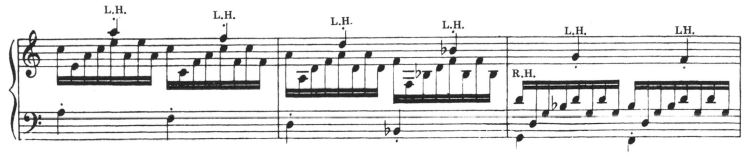

IX

S. Rachmaninoff, Op. 32. No. 9

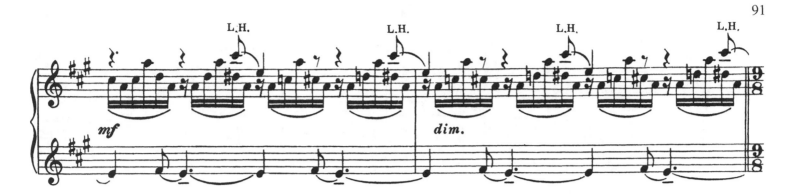

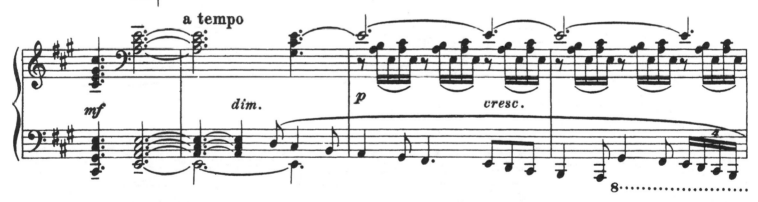

X

S.Rachmaninoff,Op.32.№10.

L'istesso tempo

a tempo, come prima

XI

S. Rachmaninoff, Op. 32. No 11.

Allegretto

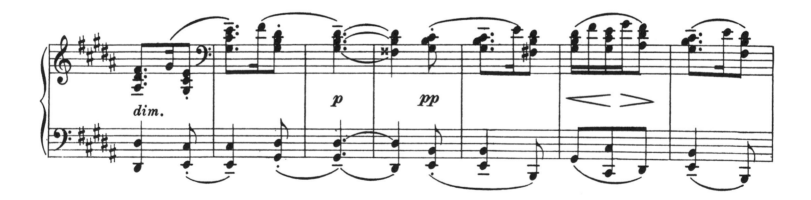

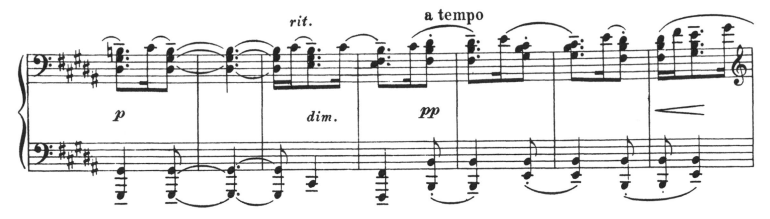

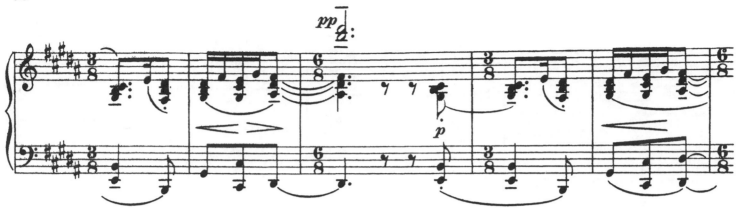

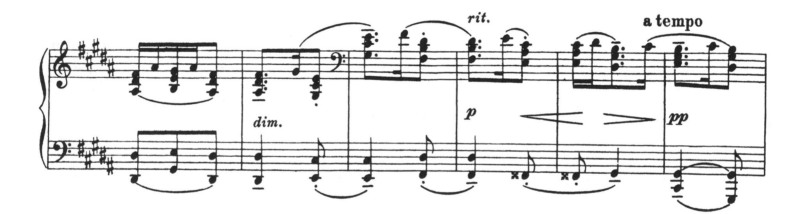

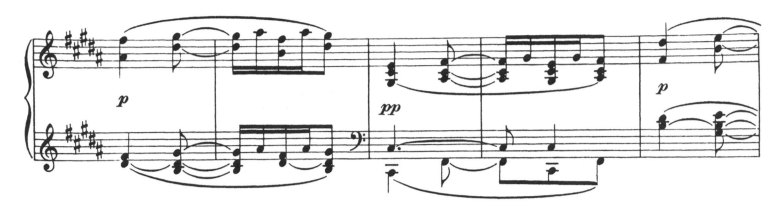

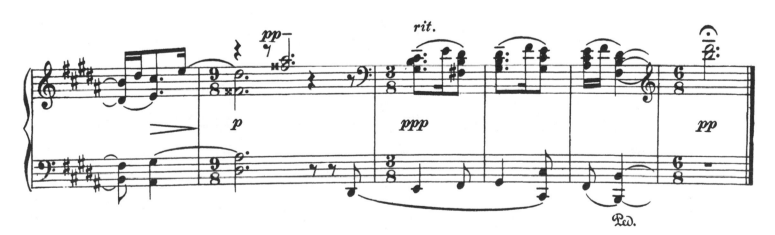

XII

S. Rachmaninoff, Op.32 № 12.

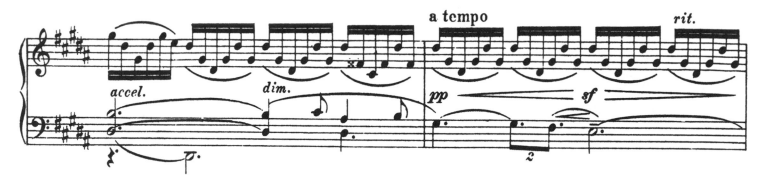

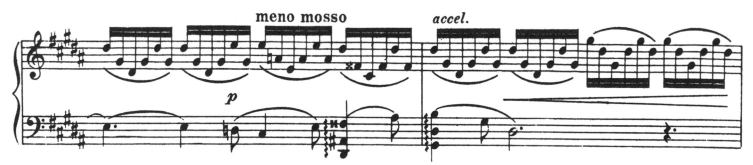

a tempo

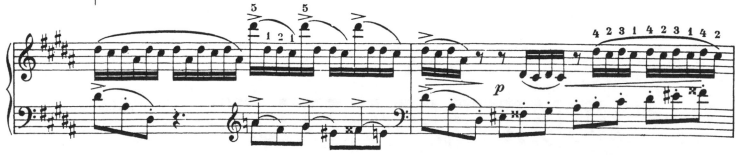

XIII

S. Rachmaninoff, Op.32 № 13.

Grave

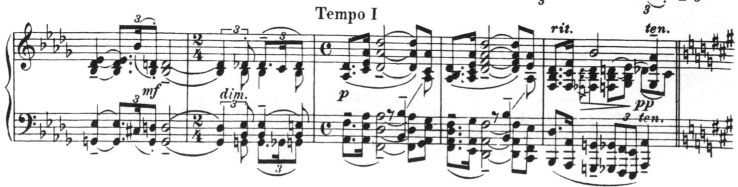

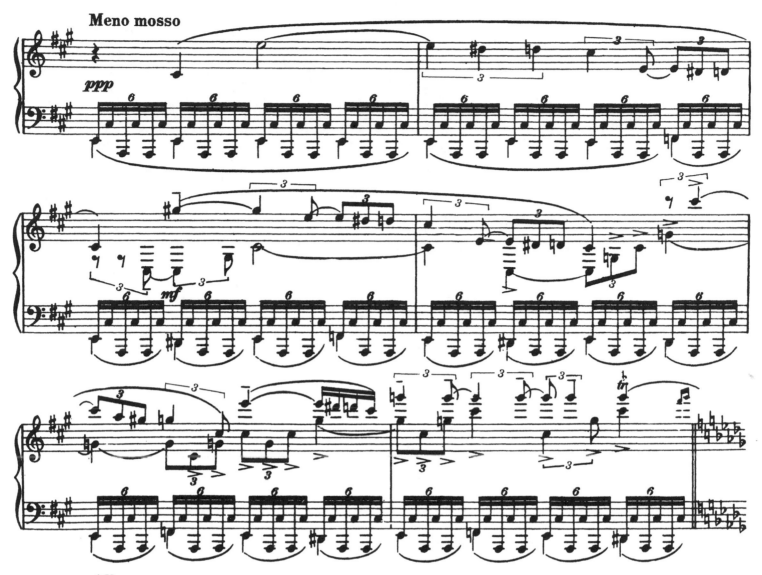

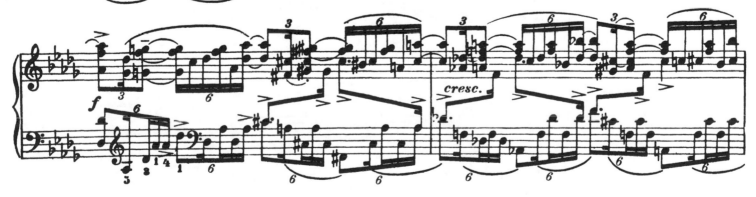

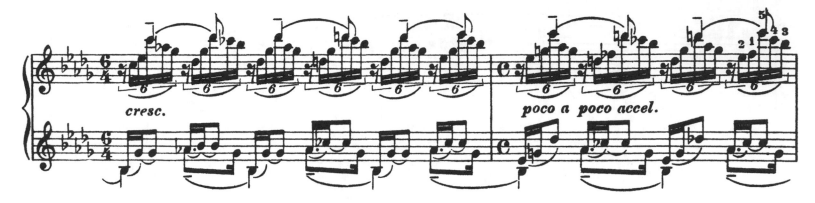

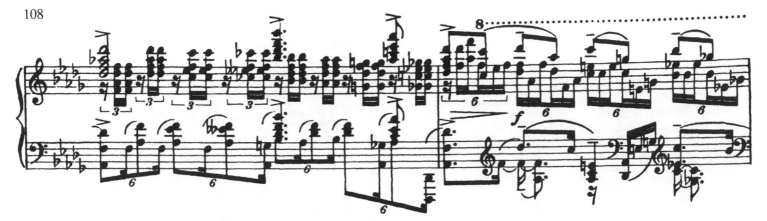